Counting to 100
6–7

Author: Lynn Huggins-Cooper
Illustrators: Emma Holt and Chris McGhie

Letts

How to use this book

Look out for these features!

IN THE ACTIVITIES

The parents' notes at the top of each activity will give you:

- a simple explanation about what your child is learning
- an idea of how you can work with your child on the activity.

This small page number guides you to the back of the book, where you will find further ideas for help.

These magic stars provide useful facts and helpful hints!

AT THE BACK OF THE BOOK

Every activity has a section for parents containing:

- further explanations about what the activity teaches
- games that can be easily recreated at home
- questions to ask your child to encourage their learning
- tips on varying the activity if it seems too easy or too difficult for your child.

You will also find the answers at the back of the book.

HELPING YOUR CHILD AS THEY USE THIS BOOK

Why not try starting at the beginning of the book and work through it? Your child should only attempt one activity at a time. Remember, it is best to learn little and often when we are feeling wide awake!

EQUIPMENT YOUR CHILD WILL NEED

- a pencil for writing
- an eraser for correcting mistakes
- coloured pencils for drawing and colouring in.

You might also like to have ready some spare paper and some collections of objects (for instance, small toys, Lego bricks, buttons...) for some of the activities.

Contents

Counting to 100

Make number cards using Board A (either by copying or cutting out). Take turns to turn up a number and place it in the correct place on Board B.

Board A

1	2	3	4	5	6	7	8	9	10
11	12	13	14	15	16	17	18	19	20
21	22	23	24	25	26	27	28	29	30
31	32	33	34	35	36	37	38	39	40
41	42	43	44	45	46	47	48	49	50
51	52	53	54	55	56	57	58	59	60
61	62	63	64	65	66	67	68	69	70
71	72	73	74	75	76	77	78	79	80
81	82	83	84	85	86	87	88	89	90
91	92	93	94	95	96	97	98	99	100

Parents 44

- This activity will familiarise your child with numbers 1–100.
- To play, copy Board A and stack the cards face down. You might set a time limit per go.

Board B

one	two	three	four	five	six	seven	eight	nine	ten
eleven	twelve	thirteen	fourteen	fifteen	sixteen	seventeen	eighteen	nineteen	twenty
twenty-one	twenty-two	twenty-three	twenty-four	twenty-five	twenty-six	twenty-seven	twenty-eight	twenty-nine	thirty
thirty-one	thirty-two	thirty-three	thirty-four	thirty-five	thirty-six	thirty-seven	thirty-eight	thirty-nine	forty
forty-one	forty-two	forty-three	forty-four	forty-five	forty-six	forty-seven	forty-eight	forty-nine	fifty
fifty-one	fifty-two	fifty-three	fifty-four	fifty-five	fifty-six	fifty-seven	fifty-eight	fifty-nine	sixty
sixty-one	sixty-two	sixty-three	sixty-four	sixty-five	sixty-six	sixty-seven	sixty-eight	sixty-nine	seventy
seventy-one	seventy-two	seventy-three	seventy-four	seventy-five	seventy-six	seventy-seven	seventy-eight	seventy-nine	eighty
eighty-one	eighty-two	eighty-three	eighty-four	eighty-five	eighty-six	eighty-seven	eighty-eight	eighty-nine	ninety
ninety-one	ninety-two	ninety-three	ninety-four	ninety-five	ninety-six	ninety-seven	ninety-eight	ninety-nine	one hundred

Counting again

My dog, Moss, shook water on the number square in the playground. Can you fill in the missing numbers?

Parents

- Filling in the numbers will help to reinforce the order of numbers up to 100.
- Refer to page 4 if your child needs extra help.

44

1	2	3	4	5	6	7	8	9	10
11	12	13	14	15	16	17	18	19	20
21	22	23	24	25	26	27	28	29	30
31	32	33	34	35	36	37	38	39	40
41	42	43	44	45	46	47	48	49	50
51	52	53	54	55	56	57	58	59	60
61	62	63	64	65	66	67	68	69	70
71	72	73	74	75	76	77	78	79	80
81	82	83	84	85	86	87	88	89	90
91	92	93	94	95	96	97	98	99	100

Counting from different points

Some number bubbles have popped!
Fill in the missing numbers in the correct order.

Parents

- This activity will help your child to become familiar with the order of numbers.
- Point out that this will help with mental arithmetic.

44

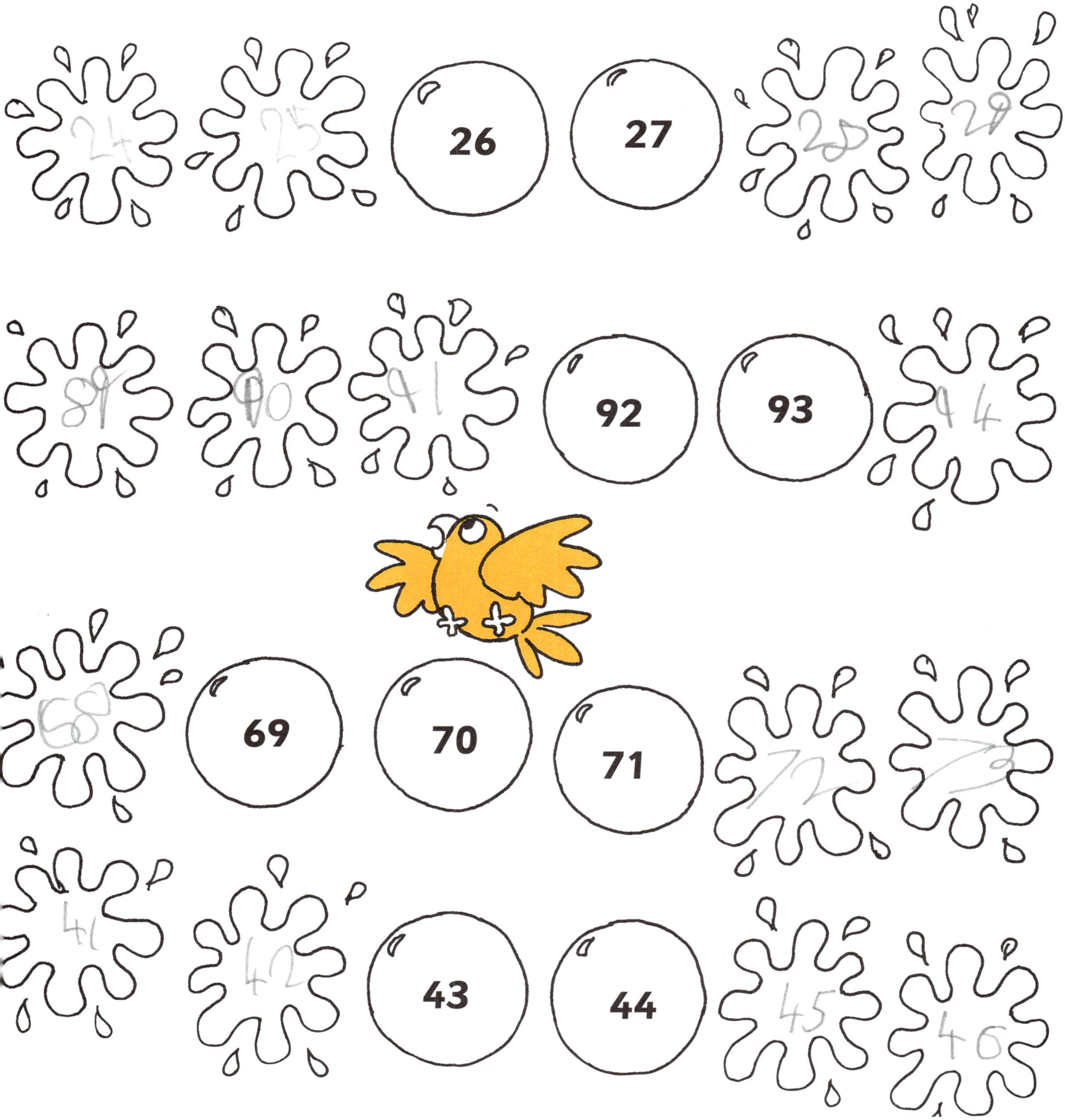

Number patterns

Hop in **tens** and colour the squares **red**.
Skip in **fives** and colour the squares **blue**.
Jump in **twos** and colour the squares **green**.

Parents

44

- Counting in twos, fives and tens will help to prepare your child for their times tables.
- Use the number square on page 4 if your child needs help.

Number matching

How many children are there in this line? 12

How many children are there in this circle? 24

Parents

44

- This activity shows that the number of objects stays the same, even when that number are rearranged.
- Use pasta shells to demonstrate this further.

Look at the children below.
Do you think that there are **more** or **less** than in the line above?

I think there are 100 children in the line.

Now count them.

How many children are there in the group? ☐

Were there **more** or **less**? ________

Counting in tens

Look at the trains.
What do you notice about the 'units' part of the number on each carriage?
Fill in the missing numbers.

Look for the number patterns!

Parents

- Counting in tens helps your child to develop strategies for answering number problems.
- Refer to the number square on page 4 if your child needs help.

45

The Magic Spell

Princess Eleanor has been turned into a toad!
Can you help to turn her back by finding the Magic Pattern?

Find the Magic Pattern

Starting at 0, count on **2** and circle the number you land on **red**.
Keep counting on in twos and colouring the numbers. Can you see the Magic Pattern?

- This activity will introduce the pattern in the 2 times table.
- Ask your child, 'What do you notice about the pattern you make?'.

Multiples of 2

Count the sea creatures and write the numbers in the boxes.

Parents 45

- Recognising multiples of 2 will help your child with tables and multiplication.
- Ask, 'What do you notice about the numbers?'.

	2
	4
	6
	8
	10

Can you see a pattern in the answers?

10 more or less

Write the numbers that come out of these number machines.

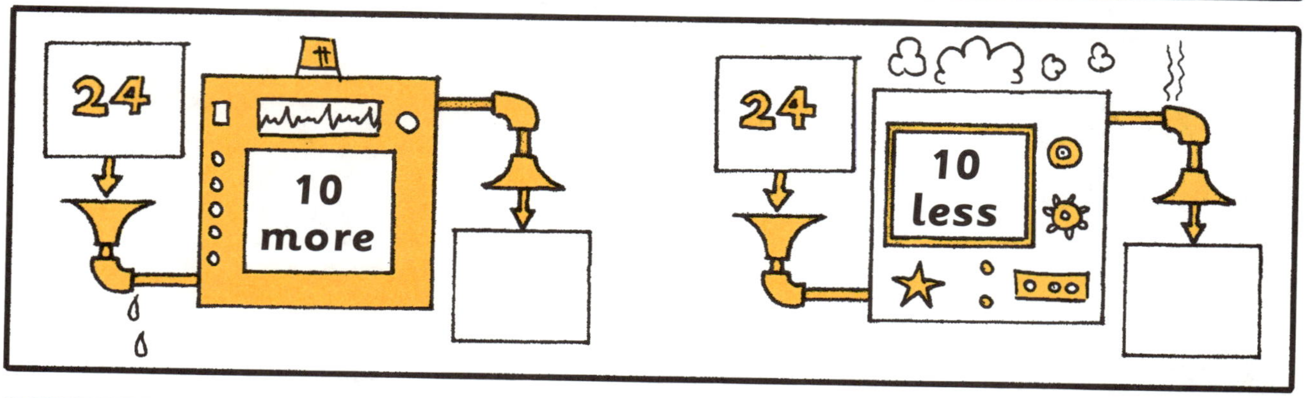

Parents

45

This activity will help your child with mental arithmetic.

They should fill in the '10 more' and '10 less' boxes.

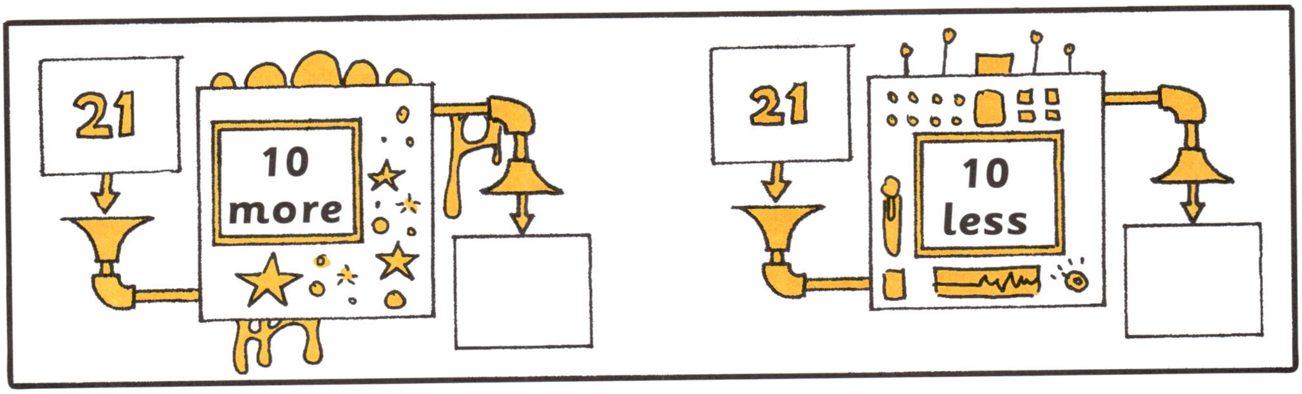

More or less

Which of these would you rather have?
Circle your answer.

15 or 25 sweets

96 or 86 chocolate coins

32 or 52 sprouts

5 + 1 = 6 ✓

21 or 73 correct sums

12 or 22 toys

46 or 64 days of measles

Parents 45

- This activity introduces the idea of 'more' and 'less', and ordering 2-digit numbers.
- Help them to decide which number is larger in each case.

Circle the biggest number.

15 25 62 26

19 29 84 63

81 18 91 94

14 98 96 41

58 21 33 10

24 42 48 84

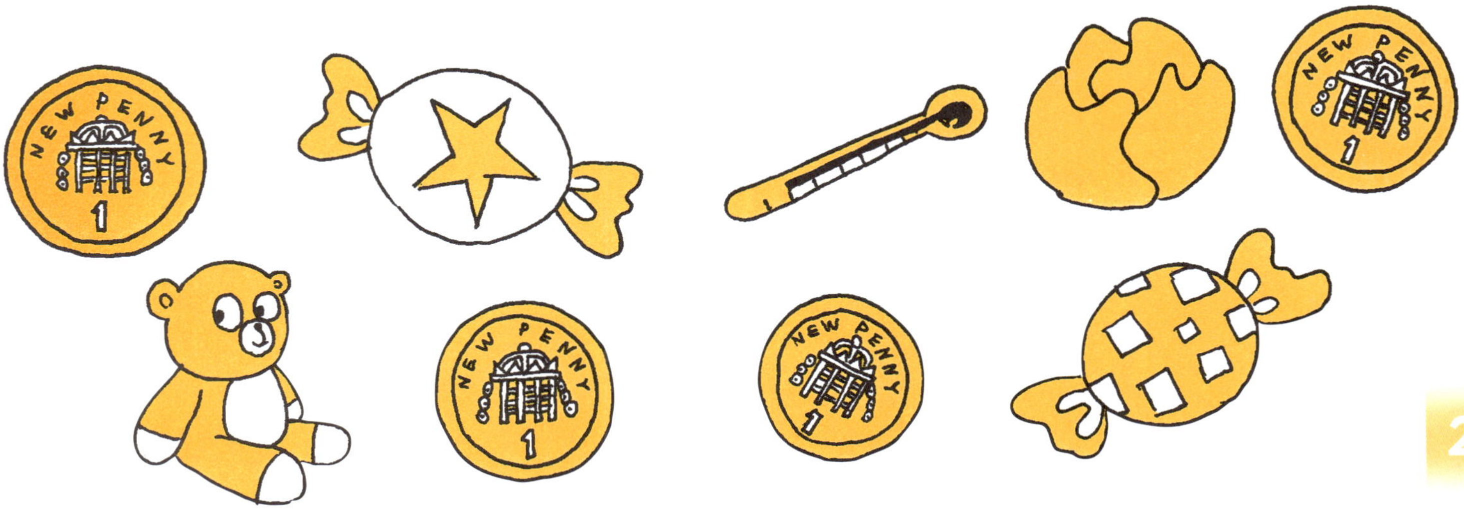

Counting in twos

Count how many ears are in each picture.

There are [ ] ears

There are 10 ears

There are 16 ears

There are 8 ears

There are 2 ears

There are 6 ears

Parents 46

- Counting in twos will help your child with multiplication, tables and division.
- Help your child to count the number of ears and write the answers.

There are 18 ears

There are 12 ears

There are 18 ears

There are 23 ears

Counting in fours

Every time the frog jumps, she moves forward **4** lily pads.
How many jumps will she take to get to the fly?
Colour each pad you land on.

- This activity will help your child to count in jumps of 4.
- Use the number line to make sure your child's first count lands on 4, then 8.

What do you notice about the pads you have coloured? Is there a pattern?

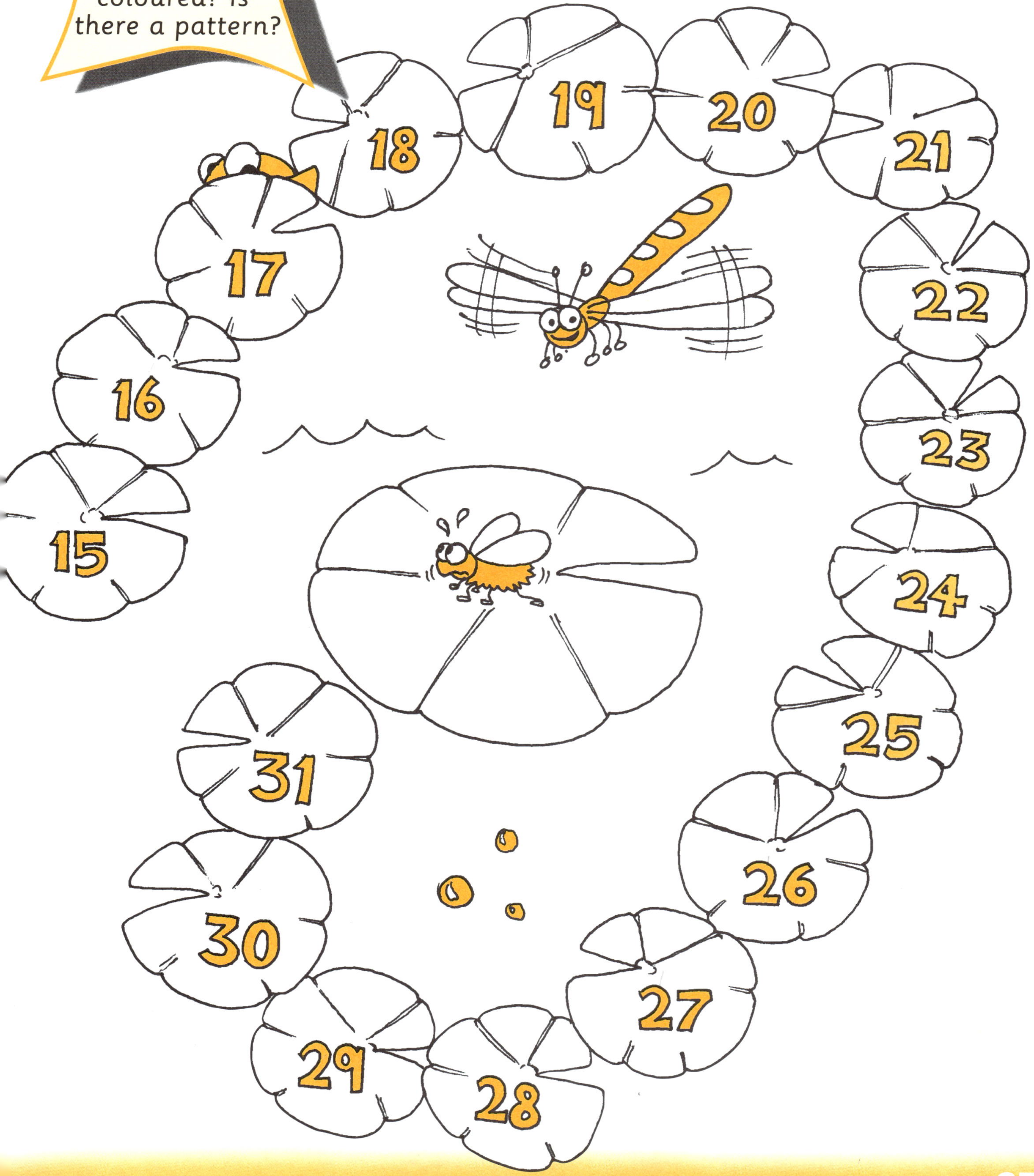

Counting in fives

Can you see any patterns in the leaves?

Sam Snail is eating some lettuce.
Count in **fives** to find out how many leaves he eats.
Colour each leaf you land on.

Parents

46

- This activity will help your child to count in fives.
- Make sure the first count lands on 5, then 10.

Recognising multiples of 5

How many eyes does each alien have? ☐ eyes

So how many eyes are there altogether in **2** rockets? ☐ eyes

In **3** rockets? ☐ eyes

Now fill in the shooting star by
counting in fives.
What do you notice about the numbers?

Parents

46

- This activity will help your child to recognise multiples of 5.
- Point out that these numbers always end in 5 or 0.

How many eyes are there In **4** rockets? ☐ eyes

In **5** rockets? ☐ eyes

In **6** rockets? ☐ eyes

Recognising multiples of 10

Colour in all the flowers containing the multiples of 10. Use Number Line Caterpillar for help.

Parents

46

- This activity will help your child to identify numbers that are multiples of 10.
- Point out that the numbers always end in 0.

What do you notice about the flowers you have coloured?

What do they all end in? ☐

Number pairs to make 100

Join each dog to a bone to make 100.
One has been done for you.

- Making number pairs to 100 will help your child's mental maths.
- Check your child's pairs all make 100.

Parents 47

Splitting 2-digit numbers

Circle each set of 10. Count how many tens you have and how many ones are left over.

How many tens? 100

How many ones? 10

How many in total? 10

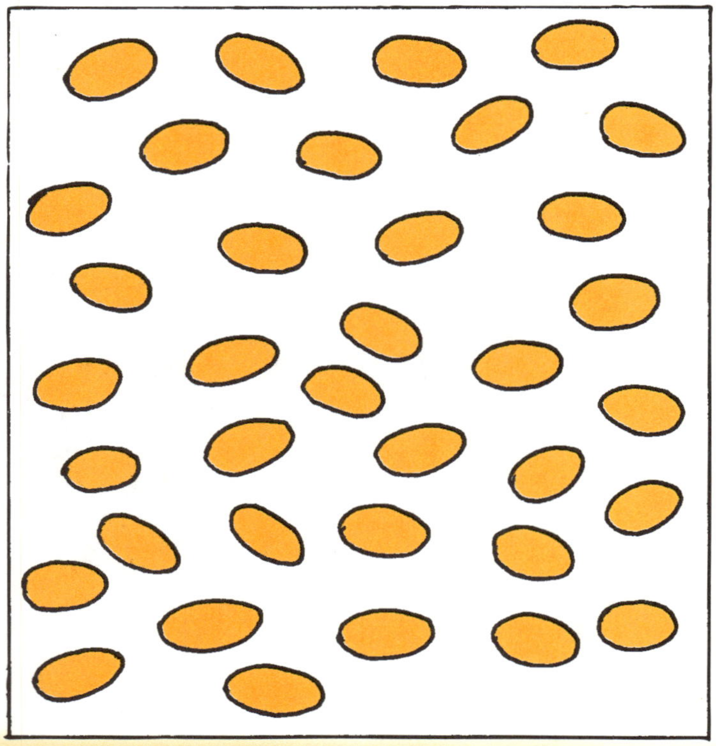

How many tens? 1

How many ones? 1

How many in total? 100

Parents

47

- This activity helps your child to 'see' a number as so many tens and so many units.
- Check your child has counted correctly and made the right conclusion.

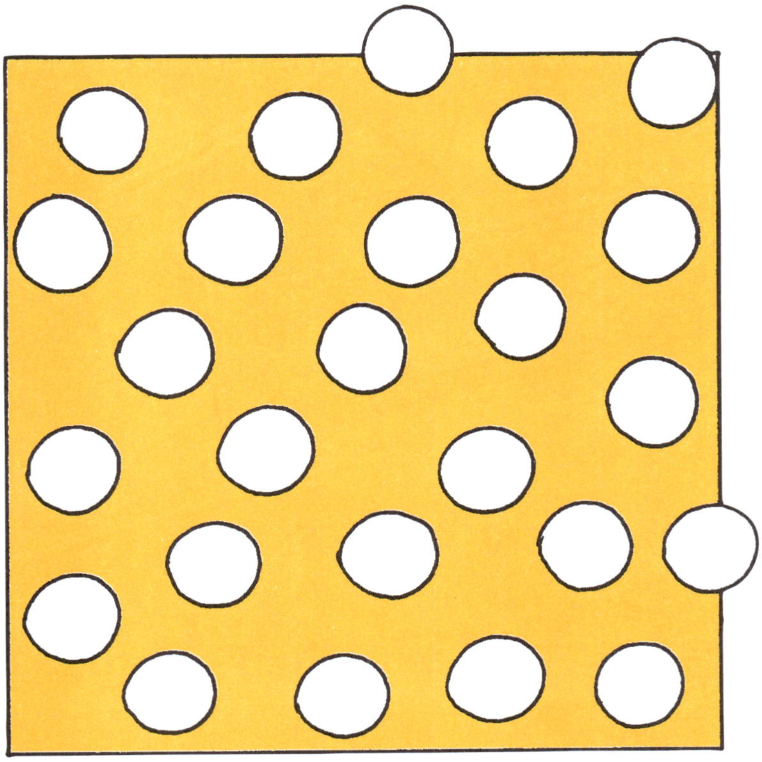

How many tens? ☐

How many ones? ☐

How many in total? ☐

How many tens? ☐

How many ones? ☐

How many in total? ☐

Place value

There are 10 ChocBomb lollies in a pack.

How many lollies are there in 3 packets and 2 lollies?

tens	units	total

How many lollies are there in 6 packets and 1 lolly?

tens	units	total

Parents

47

- This activity will help your child to 'see' numbers as sets of tens and units left over.
- Check your child has counted the objects correctly and found the right answers.

How many lollies are there in 5 packets and 4 lollies?

tens	units	total

How many lollies are there in 8 packets and 7 lollies?

tens	units	total

More place value

Write how many 10p coins and 1p coins are needed to make these totals. Draw the coins.

32p ☐ 10p coins ☐ 1p coins

64p ☐ 10p coins ☐ 1p coins

28p ☐ 10p coins ☐ 1p coins

87p ☐ 10p coins ☐ 1p coins

Parents

47

- Money is useful when teaching your child about tens and units.
- Check your child has written and drawn the correct number of coins.

92p ☐ 10p coins ☐ 1p coins

30p ☐ 10p coins ☐ 1p coins

49p ☐ 10p coins ☐ 1p coins

55p ☐ 10p coins ☐ 1p coins

Tens and units

Bookworm has eaten holes in the page!
Which number goes in each bite mark?
Can you explain why?

4	+	20	=	24
50	+	20	=	24
100	+	10	=	16
6	+	0	=	16

Parents 47

- This activity will help your child to practise tens and units.
- Listen to and praise your child's explanation, correcting where necessary.

___ + 4 = 24

5 + ___ = 24

3 + ___ = 16

___ + 5 = 16

Further activities

4–5

- Look for 'number words' in the world around you, such as in newspapers and magazines.
- Make cards with word names on one side, and the corresponding number on the other side. Encourage your child to write the number as you read the word, then check the answer together.
- Make 20 number and word dominoes out of card. Cut 20 cards. Rule a line down the middle of each card, and write a number word from 0–20 on one end. Write a number from 0–20 on the other end. Play dominoes with the cards as you would play with ordinary dominoes. Make sets for other numbers up to 100.

6–7

- Use counters or buttons to cover different numbers, and ask your child to say which numbers are covered.
- You could make a large paper number line using a strip of paper to put on the wall where your child will see it regularly.
- Point out patterns in counting, for instance, the way in which the 'units' part of each 2-digit number follows the pattern 0 1 2 3 4 5 6 7 8 9. Practise saying the numbers together, paying particular attention to twenty, thirty, forty, fifty, sixty, seventy, eighty and ninety as these number names are often difficult for young children to remember.
- *Answers: 9, 13, 25, 33, 42, 55, 61, 70, 83, 97.*

8–9

- Make a game of counting where you say a number between 0–100, and your child carries on counting.
- Play the 'Before and After' game. Say a number and ask your child to tell you the number before and after your chosen number.
- Play a game where you say 'I am thinking of a number. It is 1 more than 6. What number am I thinking of?'

  Encourage your child to make up questions for you, too.
- *Answers:* *23, 24, 25, (26, 27,) 28, 29*
89, 90, 91, (92, 93,) 94
66, 67, 68, (69, 70, 71,) 72, 73
40, 41, 42, (43, 44), 45, 46

10–11

- Write the sequence of counting in steps of 2 to 30, and look for patterns together. For example, the units part of each number follows the pattern 0 2 4 6 8.
- Extend counting beyond 30, asking your child to predict the numbers using the pattern. This 'extended counting' activity can be carried out for steps of 5 – predicting the next sequence of numbers using the pattern 0/5/0/5.

12–13

- Many practical examples of counting a group of objects as they are rearranged will be needed before your child will understand that the number will always stay the same.
- Use two equal groups of buttons, sweets, shells or any small objects, say 20 in total. Count the objects together as you lay them out in two equal lines. Ask your child how many objects are in each line. Emphasise that the quantities are the same.

  Rearrange the objects from one line into a group and ask your child which set has more. Children will often say the line of objects as it looks 'bigger'. Repeat with other numbers of objects.
- *Answers: There are 24 children in all three groups.*

14–15

- Make a number line marked in tens up to 100. Ask questions such as 'Can you count on in tens from 60? From 30?'
- Look for number patterns together, for instance, that the number pattern counting in tens from 10–100 is the same as the familiar 1–10 pattern, with a 0 on the end to show that the numbers are 'tens' rather than 'units'.
- *Answers: 33, 43, 53, 63, 73, 83, 93*
  28, 38, 48, 58, 68, 78, 88
  24, 34, 44, 54, 64, 74, 84
  32, 42, 52, 62, 72, 82, 92
  19, 29, 39, 49, 59, 69, 79

16–17

- Using the number line, say to your child, 'The red numbers are called even numbers, and the green numbers are called odd numbers. Even numbers make sets of 2 with none left over. Odd numbers do not.'
- Demonstrate this with sweets, perhaps in the context of sharing out. Ask your child whether numbers are odd or even, giving them the opportunity to check with real objects.
- To extend the activity further, you could point out the interesting fact that even numbers end in 0 2 4 6 8. Encourage your child to test this theory with 2-digit numbers up to 30.

18–19

- Count in twos with your child, encouraging them to go as far as they can.
- Look for number patterns in multiples of 2 when they are written down. Compare the sequence of numbers with the sequence of even numbers identified in the activity on pages 16–17.

- Make links between the two series of numbers by explaining that even numbers can be shared exactly by 2, as can multiples of 2.
- *Answers: 2 octopusses, 4 jellyfish, 6 starfish, 8 fish 10 shells.*

20–21

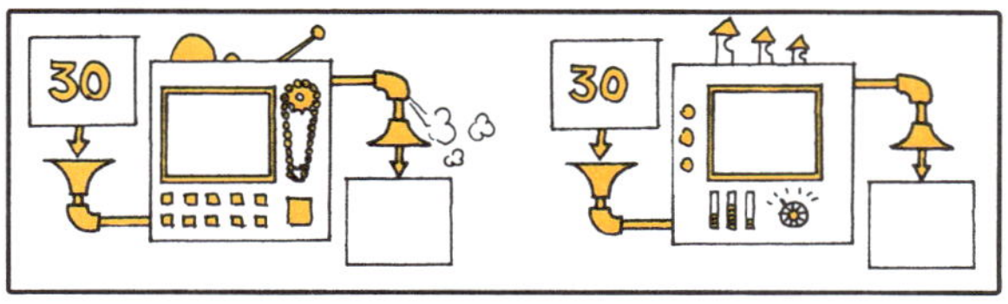

- Make a set of cards with the numbers 1–100. (Cereal packet card, or cut up pieces of paper are fine for this activity.) Ask your child to find '10 less than 41… 10 more than 67… 10 more than 8… ' Your child should find the correct card to answer the question.
- *Answers: 30: 40, 20; 24: 34, 14; 83: 93, 73; 19: 29, 9; 42: 52, 32; 59: 69, 49; 84: 94, 74; 21: 31, 11.*

22–23

- Use the cards you made for the activity on pages 4–5 for this activity. Select three or four cards and ask your child to put them in order from the smallest to the largest, or vice versa.
- Ask them to explain how they know – talking about working out in mathematics is a vital part of a child's exploration and development.

- *Answers: Talk about your child's answers, using 'more' and 'less'.*
  Biggest numbers: 62, 84, 94, 98, 58, 84.

Further activities

24–25

- Ask your child to see how far they can get counting in steps of 2.
- Ask questions such as, 'If there are two wings on each bat, how many wings will eight bats have?'
- Count 'twos' in the environment, such as eyes, ears, legs and arms.
- *Answers: 2 ears; 10, 16, 14, 12 ears; 8, 2, 6, 20 ears.*

26–27

- Write the sequence of counting in steps of 4 and look for patterns together, for instance, in the order of 'units': 0 4 8 2 6.
- Ask your child to predict larger 'steps of 4'. Practise counting in fours orally to remind your child of the sequence of numbers.

  This sequence is, of course, the sequence for the 4 times table. Ask your child questions such as. 'If a table has four legs, and I have three tables, how many legs are there altogether?'

  Answers: She takes 8 jumps.

28–29

- Chant with your child the number sequence of counting in steps of 5 to 30. This sequence is, of course, the sequence for the 5 times table.

  Ask your child questions such as 'If a plant has five leaves and I have two plants, how many leaves are there altogether?'
- Say a number in the sequence, such as 25, and ask your child to count backwards or forwards in fives.
- *Answers: He eats 6 leaves.*

30–31

- Use 5p coins to encourage your child to count in fives. Give them piles of 5p coins and ask them how many pence there are in each pile altogether.
- Make rubbings of groups of 5p coins with your child by placing a coin under paper and rubbing with a pencil. Ask them to count the value of the groups of coins by counting in steps of 5.
- *Answers: Each alien has 5 eyes, 10 eyes, 15 eyes, 20 eyes, 25 eyes and 30 eyes. Numbers: 10, 15, 20, 25, 30, 35, 40, 45, 50, 55, 60.*

32–33

- Write a series of 2-digit numbers such as 43, 67 and 80, on a piece of paper. Ask your child to draw a circle around all the multiples of 10.
- Use the cards made for pages 20–21 to play 'Tens'. Shuffle the cards, and deal them to two or three players. Each player takes a turn to place a card face up on the pile. When a multiple of 10 appears, the first player to shout 'Tens' collects the cards. Play continues until one person holds the majority of cards or a player loses them all.
- *Answers: 10, 90, 30, 70, 40, 100.*

34–35

- Make number pair cards. Cut 22 cards from card, such as a cereal packet, and write the following numbers on the cards twice each: 0, 10, 20, 30, 40, 50, 60, 70, 80, 90 and 100. Lay out one set of cards 0–100 in random order on the floor. Ask your child to pick the number cards to make '100 pairs' from the second set of cards. These should be placed next to the matching card from the first set.

- *Answers: 0/100, 10/90, 20/80, 30/70, 40/60, 50/50, 60/40, 70/30, 80/20, 90/10, 0/100.*

36–37

- Make a set of 9 cards measuring 6cm long. Write 10, 20, 30, 40, 50, 60, 70, 80 and 90 on the cards. Tell your child that these cards stand for 'tens'. Now make a set of 9 cards measuring 3cm long but the same width as the first cards. Write 1, 2, 3, 4, 5, 6, 7, 8 and 9 on the cards. Tell your child that these cards stand for 'units'.
- You are going to play a game with the cards. Say a number such as '68'. Your child should find the card showing 60 and the card showing 8. The 'unit' card is placed on top of the 'ten' card so that the 0 on the 10-card is hidden. Encourage your child to tell you that 68 is made up from 6 tens and 8 units.
- *Answers: 1 ten, 0 units = 10 biscuits; 3 tens, 6 units = 36 beads; 2 tens, 5 units = 25 beads; 1 ten, 8 units = 18 sweets.*

38–39

- Make up other scenarios for this problem, such as packets of crayons in packs of tens. Ask your child questions, such as, 'How many crayons are there in two packets and three extra? How many crayons in five packets and one extra?' and so on.
- *Answers: 32 lollies, 61 lollies, 54 lollies, 87 lollies.*

40–41

- Use real money to extend this activity. Draw two columns on a piece of A4 paper. Write 'tens' and 'ones' at the top of the columns. Ask your child to make a series of amounts with play or real 10p coins and 1p coins, such as, say 'Show me 36p in tens and ones'. Your child should place the appropriate number of tens and ones in the correct columns.
- *Answers: 3x10p coins, 2x1p; 6x10p, 4x1p; 2x10p, 8x1p; 8x10p, 7x1p; 9x10p, 2x1p; 3x10, 0x1p; 4x10p, 9x1p; 5x10p, 5x1p.*

42–43

- Use the cards made for the activity on pages 33–33 to extend this activity. Make two extra cards showing + and =. Set out cards to make a sum, for instance, 10 + ? = 15. Your child has to choose the correct card to go in the gap to balance the sum (in this case, 5).
- *Answers: 20, 4, 6, 10, 20, 19, 13, 11.*

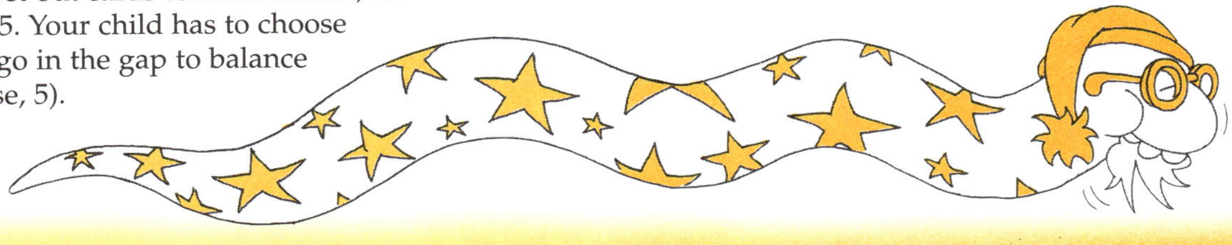

Celebration!

I can count to 100.

I can count in twos, fours and fives.

I can count in tens.

I recognise 10 more and 10 less.

I can break numbers into tens and units.